A PILGRIMAGE TO ICELAND

by

John C. Wilhelmsson

A PILGRIMAGE TO ICELAND

A PILGRIMAGE TO ICELAND

Chaos To Order Publishing

San Jose, California

c2op.com

A Pilgrimage To Iceland

Copyright © 2013 by John C. Wilhelmsson

All rights reserved.

ISBN: 0988656329

ISBN-13: 978-0988656321

A Pilgrimage To Iceland

Published March 19, 2013.

The Feast of Saint Joseph.

A PILGRIMAGE TO ICELAND

"Though your health is ailing all is not lost,

Your sons can swell your pride,

Your brave kinsman,

Your fine cattle,

Your work well done."

The Saying of the Vikings

A PILGRIMAGE TO ICELAND

	Introduction	1
1)	The Journey Begins	5
2)	Becoming a Pilgrim	11
3)	Touched by the Past	15
4)	I Have Finally Arrived	21
5)	That are Bubby!	25
6)	The Golden Circle	45
7)	The Mystery of Fatherhood	53
8)	A Talk With Harry	65
9)	Accepting the Invitation	75
10)	Christ is Present in Akureyri	83
11)	The Family Gathering	95
12)	He Give Gift!	105
	Epilogue	115

A PILGRIMAGE TO ICELAND

x

A Pilgrimage To Iceland

INTRODUCTION

I wrote this story as a journal during my first visit to Iceland in 2001. I had planned to make this trip together with my father on the fifty-year anniversary of his departure from Iceland, yet he died rather suddenly in late 1999 so I set out on my own pilgrimage to Iceland in order to honor his memory.

The particular path I followed while in Iceland was a trip all the way around the island on "The Ring Road." It is a journey often made by Icelanders who wish to rediscover their past and grow closer to their land and country so the use of the term "Pilgrimage" to describe such a journey is not far out of place.

Yet my first trip to Iceland held an even deeper meaning for me and my family as we sought to mourn the loss of our father. And since I am from a rather large family, I decided to keep a journal along the way so I might share all that I might find.

In deciding whether to share such a work many considerations came to mind. Was it just a personal story? Something that might have great meaning to me yet not to others. Was it just a family story? A story that I had been right to share among those closest to me, yet which should really go no further? In the end I decided that, while this story is about a particular time and place and family, it is also about many universal themes. Thus, sharing it with others was the right and appropriate thing to do.

I think this process of understanding the universal themes which underlie our own experience is very much akin to learning how to make a spiritual interpretation of the events in our lives. And while some might discount such interpretations as being too subjective and emotional, I would argue that such interpretations are, in reality, the things that make us most authentically human.

Iceland's land and culture are among the most beautiful and pristine in the world. While all of the recent attention it has been getting as a travel destination is welcome, they also feature their own dangers. For the attitude of a tourist is to take things in, while the attitude of a pilgrim is to be open to receive. And any land and culture, no matter how rugged or strong, cannot long survive if all those who visit it seek only to take.

   Therefore, in a very important way this book has now become a plea that there might be less tourists, and more pilgrims in Iceland! And that by being truly open to receive, those who encounter Iceland might be truly blessed by its people, land, and culture. And by the great sense of peace this land of fire and ice often engenders in the souls of those who seek to receive it.

CHAPTER ONE

THE JOURNEY BEGINS

My journey begins sitting here in the quite mundane yet familiar San Jose, California, Airport Terminal C. Farewells have always been hard for me yet this time even moreso as I have a deep realization that this journey, my Icelandic adventure, is really more of a pilgrimage. And any real pilgrimage is not just an experience, but an encounter that changes lives. So now I ask myself, "What do I seek from this encounter?" I believe that I seek to more fully know myself through better understanding my past. This is why Iceland is so important to me. It holds some great mystery of who I really am. Not just the place, but the people and culture as well. I believe that God has given me this opportunity as a great grace—a grace to more authentically know myself which is, in reality, an opportunity to better know Christ who lives within me (despite all of my shortcomings and flaws).

As I begin this adventure in this mundane yet familiar place I have many questions. What will I find? How will it change me? And, perhaps the greatest question, "How will coming to a better understanding of myself through knowing the past help me truly enter into communion with others?"

The trip got off to a bit of a rough start when our airplane lost cabin pressure and we were forced to land in San Francisco. This travail was actually welcomed by me because everything had seemed like it was happening too easily. And I believe that the good things in life should never come easily.

My father instilled in me this sort or an ethic of hard work at an early age. For during my first year of junior high school I had gotten into a good deal of trouble. So much trouble that I was sent to live and work with my father the following summer.

My father was a machinist who made parts for the great turbines which powered Navy ships. He was no stranger to ships as his father Vilhelm

Jonsson had been a Chief Engineer and at one time owned several fishing ships on Iceland. As a young man, my father had worked aboard some of these ships. There was already in fact a strong tradition of father-son work in our family that one of the great tales of the family history spoke to.

    As a young man, perhaps about my age at the time, my father had been sent out to sea to work with "Grandpa Willy" on one of his ships. Being the engineer's son had hardly afforded him easy duty as he was given the job of stoking the boiler. Well at one point while shoveling the coal into the boiler my father's clothing caught on fire! He then rushed up on deck and jumped over the side of the ship into the sea in order to extinguish the flames. This act did put out the flames, yet my father got a bad infection from being in the cold sea water which caused him to eventually lose most of his hearing in one ear.

    With such an auspicious history of father son work in the family I had no idea about what to expect during my summer at the machine shop. Yet Daddy made the plan clear to me from the start. I would get up 5:30am and come to work with him every day. I would be paid $1 per hour, 50 cents from him and 50 cents from the shop owner, which would give me a paycheck of $40 per week. The $40 per week would be spent in the following way each month: The first week's $40 would pay my rent because a man should always contribute to his household. The second week's $40 would be deposited into a savings account which would be open in my name because a man should always try and save his money. And the rest of the month's wages would be for me to spend as I chose as this is the privilege of being a working man. The lessons of a father to his son that summer still resonate in my life today. And the good feeling of working hard for your wages, whatever they might be, gave me a sense of dignity and self-respect which have shaded the rest of my life in so many ways. Thank you, Daddy, for that first summer working together. You gave me all of the lessons a father could hope to give his son and I am still benefiting from them today.

A PILGRIMAGE TO ICELAND

CHAPTER TWO

BECOMING A PILGRIM

No good thing in life should come easily and there were more rough times today. I barely slept last night in the Mount Vernon Inn. I don't find the people in this part of Baltimore to be too friendly so I decided to book into an Inner Harbor Hotel so I will have a comfortable bed to sleep in and a nice safe place to stay. The only problem with such accommodations are the inherent temptations within them.

I am about as imperfect as my journey so far—lots of ups and downs yet I usually reach my destination. Yet I have come to see these imperfections more and more, or the fact of their existence, as being just another type of a cross to carry. I just hope it gets lighter as time goes by.

The grace of God works in such mysterious ways. I shut myself up in my hotel room today, yet I have learned so much. The local public broadcasting station had a show on about the play "Les Miserables." I have known of the existence of this play for quite some time yet never have seen it, or even known its story, until recently. The lead character in the play is a man named Jean Val Jean. He is a man who is dealt some very unfortunate and harsh circumstances in life and, thus, loses his faith in God only to regain it later through the dramatic actions of a very holy man.

The greatest thing about this particular show for me was that, towards the end of it, they paraded the actors who have played Jean Vel Jean out on stage from all of the different countries where the play has been done. They came from all around the world. There must have been at least 20 of them, and one of the last ones to come out was from Iceland! It was as if to say that the message of God's grace, which is found so profoundly within this play, is in Iceland as well. That Iceland is a place touched by God's grace!

As I look back today, I see this as a key moment. For I was beginning to realize that my journey to Iceland was not just that of a tourist seeking to see the sites but that of a pilgrim seeking to find God's grace. Not just that of a person looking to take things in but rather that of a person hoping to receive. This fundamental distinction is often forgotten in the modern world yet something the ancients knew well.

    The word *ratio* means something which is achieved by human effort while the word *intellectus* means something which is given by God's grace. Thus, the words "rationality" and "intellect" are not interchangeable but two very separate and distinct aspects of a complete human thought process. And the highest moment of this process is not when we study and dissect things through our own efforts but, rather, the moment when we receive a vision by grace! Thus, the choice of being either a tourist or a pilgrim is a reflection of the greater basic human choice of being either a person who only knows how to take by human effort or being a person who is open to receive by divine grace! And it was only in realizing this distinction, and making a choice for the latter, that my pilgrimage to Iceland could truly begin.

CHAPTER THREE
TOUCHED BY THE PAST

Everything I have done thus far has been focused on arriving in Iceland as safely and as freshly as possible. I hardly saw anything of Baltimore, yet I don't really care. It was just a dangerous way station and obstacle for me in reaching my real destination. However, this conservative game plan has its own pitfalls. When can I step out from behind my bulwarks and live? This is now both a figurative and literal question.

I just checked my bags and got my boarding pass for the flight to Iceland. I feel very emotional right now. As I was in line the two men behind me began speaking Icelandic and all of these memories of my father began rushing back. It is not a sad emotion, yet it did make me want to cry. As I stood around the Icelanders in line, and saw the Icelanders behind the counter, I realized that I have never really had the chance to know my own people and culture.

I think that is why I have always had so much

trouble feeling like I was an authentic part of a community. I have never really known "the line of my people." That is why my own strained family situation right now does not bother me a great deal. For I have not really felt part of a family for a long time in any case. And I do not think that it is about believing that your culture or ethnicity is better, it is more just about knowing who you are. And I do not believe I have ever known who I am in the most profound and important ways.

Now, in this moment of revelation, I have come to realize that I am not really going on this trip as a gift to honor my father, but my father is the one who is giving me the gift! The one last great gift he wished to give me of really coming to know myself on the deepest level. So just as with God the Father, who has in all ways given me everything, even the very will to wish to serve Him, the gifts of my human father precede and are greater than mine. I had often in the past been under the false impression that my efforts were the more important ones. Yet now I have learned that I do not need to strive as much to give as I simply need to open myself up to more authentically receive. This Truth has set me free (John 8:32).

Just a few minutes to boarding now. Our airplane is named "Fanndis" and I took the first picture with my new camera of her. Everyone is much more quiet now. I am sitting across from a father and son who remind me very much of Daddy and I when I was a teenager working with him in the machine shop. The son has a very American English accent with hair down to his shoulders, just like mine at that age, while the father has an Icelandic accent much like Dad's.

So much is here for me just by watching and listening. Just to hear the voices and see the faces carries so much emotion and meaning! The Icelanders are all so different, yet they feel so very familiar. I can only think of those words of Saint Peter, "How good it is to be here" (Luke 9:33).

As our flight rides towards its destination the light on the horizon grows brighter and brighter. Iceland is a land of light! And I can't help now but to believe that some of my own darkness will come to be bathed in Iceland's light.

I prayed for God's will to be done and now I am sitting next to a very good Catholic gentleman named Randal. He is a lawyer in Washington DC. I see his presence as providential in that in my wish to discover who I am on this pilgrimage a strong Catholic gentleman is the first person whom I meet.

I have often thought about whether the most important thing in life is human effort or divine grace. My father use to say that "God helps those who help themselves." And certainly, to succeed at anything important in life requires hard work. Yet for me the most special times in life have always been the ones where I sensed I was walking in God's providence. Speeding toward Iceland now I feel I am just where God wants me to be!

A PILGRIMAGE TO ICELAND

CHAPTER FOUR
I HAVE FINALLY ARRIVED

I have finally arrived! I walked into Reykjavik early today to see the downtown. The wind was howling, and it was so cold that my ears hurt, yet I was so excited that I really didn't care. I first went to see the great Lutheran Cathedral, which dominates the skyline, and then walked about the town. I bought some books for my brother and the beautiful blonde girl in the bookstore said "Gooan dag" to me when I walked in thinking I was an Icelander. [The Icelanders taking me for one of their own happened over and over again. It gave me a sort of mystical feeling like I had entered into a reality which had been meant to be mine. Like a long-forgotten destiny being reawakened in my soul].

I did not really eat a decent meal today in all of the excitement and I am getting a sore throat and a head cold. I can't help but think of Grandma and how she would have taken care of me and fed me well at the first sign of sickness. She even used to hide vitamins in our oatmeal to keep us kids healthy were all little. Woman really serve to protect and nourish men in so many ways that we often take for granted. Having a good woman in your life is a very important thing.

As I came back from town, I stopped into the Icelandair office for some assistance with my itinerary. A woman named Vilma helped me. She treated me so well and made me feel so much at home that she reminded me of my Aunt Bara. As a child, Aunt Bara would always welcome me into her room, at Grandma's house, and let me sit down on the couch next to her and watch "The Lawrence Welk Show." I like to watch the reruns of that show on the public broadcasting station now because they remind me of those times.

So many things touch me here. I am reminded of the last generation of the family and how I loved them and miss them and wish I had treated them all better while they were still here. They live on in my heart and they live on here in Iceland in their, our, people.

I wandered into a shop today where knitting

supplies are sold. A nice lady was there, and she realized, almost immediately, that I had not intended to come to such a place. Yet she was very kind and understanding toward me and offered to let me stay as long as I wanted to in order to warm up. She told me that the weather had been bad all May and that she could hardly wait for summer. I bought a picture of Iceland that can be knitted together for my sister Christine. She greatly enjoys cross-stitching so I hope she will like it.

    This is just one example of how kind and helpful the people are toward one another here in Iceland. I was looking at my map today, with a quite perplexed look on my face, and this little boy came up to me and offered to help. He spoke to me in Icelandic, just like the girl at the bookstore, so we could not communicate well yet it was still a wonderful act. He looked so much like me that he could have been my son and his kindness made me feel like we are a part of the same family.

CHAPTER FIVE
THAT ARE BUBBY!

Today was Reykjavik's first day of summer splendor. After picking up my rental car and checking out of the Hotel Loftleider, I went to the Apotek (Chemist) to get some medicine for my sore throat and cold. Here in Iceland, you do not just walk up to the shelf and pull down the medicine you want. You actually speak to a chemist and let them know your problem so they can give you what you need. The lady who helped me did not understand English well, but she gave me these great cough drops called "Strepsils" that worked so well that I came back later for more.

The lady reminded me a little of Grandma, or as she was known "Imba." Icelandic people love nicknames, so Grandma is "Imba" and Daddy is "Bubby." My cousin here in Iceland goes by "Gully" and my great uncle by "Haddi." My Aunt Swan told me to just tell people that I am Bubby's son and they all will know just who I am!

I went to the Reykjavik Botanical Gardens after I got my medicine. Many young people were there working to get the place in beautiful shape for the summer. Iceland is located just below the Arctic Circle so one does not expect to find beautiful gardens full of thousands of species of blooming flowers. Yet here in Iceland what many other people might take for granted is worked hard for and treasured. And not just by the old and the wise people, but by the very young. [And these Gardens would not even turn out to be the most impressive I encountered].

Next, I headed south, looking for the Kentucky Fried Chicken restaurant I had seen on the way in from Keflavik Airport. I had heard great things about the KFC restaurants in Iceland from my relatives, but I could not find this particular one. Instead, I found a little corner market that sold fried chicken. I love to eat fried chicken when I have a cold.

Downtown Reykjavik was my next stop. I wanted to find the Arni Magnusson Institute which has many of the old Saga manuscripts on display. It took a while to get used to driving in Iceland. They drive on the same side of the road as in the US, yet the roads and signs are quite different. The roundabouts were the most fun! One roundabout even had a statue that looked like a huge Viking sword stuck in the ground in the middle of it. Sometimes, because it was so fun, I would just go round and round a few times!

It was difficult to find the Arni Magnusson Institute on the map, but I finally did. They had a special "1000 Years of Christianity in Iceland" display still running from last year. The place is not just a museum but an actual school, too, and many young people were all around. The young lady at the front counter was very nice to me. I was all dressed up in my turtleneck and dark brown jacket, my "Professor Outfit," so maybe she thought I was a visiting scholar.

After I went through the main exhibit, I went across the hall to where many of the very old copies of the Sagas are on display. Afterward, I went back to the front counter and bought a nice poster of St. George and the Dragon and some postcards with an inscription of Jesus on the Cross with Mary and the Apostle John at his feet.

After having seen all the old copies of the Sagas I also bought a new copy of the Edda Saga so I could begin to prepare myself for the visit to *Reykholt*. It is the home of my ancestor Snorri Sturluson and I plan to go see it toward the end of my journey. Knowing that I come from the line of Snorri has become a source of great pride for me, so the visit to *Reykholt* is greatly anticipated.

Then I decided to return to the Reykjavik downtown shopping district once again, where I had been the day before, and it was like night and day compared to that first visit. The sun had finally come out in Reykjavik after a May full of rain and cold wind and the streets were bustling with people full of the implicit joy such an event brings. Reykjavik was in all its glory!

I needed to pick up a map of "*Reykjavik og Nagrenni*" (Reykjavik and the surrounding area) so I could find Cousin Gully's house later that night. I had called her on the phone on Tuesday, my first phone call while in Iceland, and she had invited me to come over for dinner at 6:00 pm that very night. After dinner we were to go and meet Haddi and Palina. Well, I could have walked two blocks to get my map, but it was all so glorious being there with all of the joy and energy of the people and the sunshine, walking along a route taken by all the line of my people, that I decided to walk all the way down to the little bookstore I had visited the day before.

After I got to the bookstore and found my map, I walked all the way back along the same route savoring every sight and sound of the happy Icelanders enjoying their first day of summer splendor. When I reached the spot where I had parked my car, I remembered that an old cemetery was close by, and I thought about Grandfather. I had never met my Grandfather Vilhelm Jonsson, or "Willy," as he was known in the family, but Dad had told me many stories about him. About how he had been one of only two men in all of Iceland who held the engineer's certificate to take out the big fishing ships. And great tales like when he had brought a ship that all on shore thought lost through a great storm by having the crew throw every piece of wood on it into the boiler. I knew Daddy would have visited Grandpa Willy's grave, so I became determined to visit it myself in his place.

So, I put some more money in the parking meter and set off for the old cemetery near the *Tjornin*. Once I found it, all the gates I went by said *"Bannao"* (forbidden), so I began to think that I would not be able to go in. Then I, finally, came to the main gate, it was all the way over on the other side from where I had started, yet I was still hesitant to go in out of respect for all the deceased Icelanders within. I suddenly had this great realization that every person who lay in that cemetery was really an important part of me. That it was sacred and holy place. However, I decided that if I pulled my Rosary out of my pocket and began praying things would most likely be fine.

After I had walked a fair way down the main path, I saw an older woman who was being called out to by a beautiful young lady, "Mamie, Mamie." Then they both went into this building which seemed like some sort of an office. The young woman was tall and strong of limb with blond hair that fell down past her shoulders. She was wearing a modest jogging suit type outfit and was, obviously, dressed for some sort of hard physical work. Although her face was beautiful, it also had a look of strength about it which matched the rest of her body. She was noble and strong and seemed to have the ability to totally focus all her person on the task at hand.

    As I observed her and her mother helping another person, I saw that her father was there helping, too. What a joy to have dad, mom, and daughter all working together as a family. After they were done helping the other person, all their attention became so focused on me that I did not even feel the need to exchange greetings with them in order to gain it. I simply told them that I was looking for my grandfather and asked if they could find anyone named "Wilhelmsson" [I later realized that "Wilhelmsson" was actually spelled "Vilhelmsson" in Icelandic and that Grandpa Willy's name is actually "Jonsson"]. Then, despite the fact that I had the wrong name, they all began to generously help me.

The daughter was particularly helpful, yet we could not turn up any person named "Wilhelmsson" or "Vilhelmsson" in the cemetery. But she was not done attempting to help me yet so; next, she asked me if I knew where the "Pearl" was. Well, as far as I was concerned, I was looking at "The Pearl" of all women standing right in front of me but, like the unromantic fellow I sometimes am, I just said "no."

Then she offered to show me where "The Pearl" was, and I quickly agreed. So we began walking together down the path I had taken into the cemetery. I made some small talk about my travels so far that day which she replied to. Her English was good enough, yet she spoke it in a simple kind of a way through a thick Icelandic accent that made her voice simply unforgettable. When we came to the gate I had come in through, we stepped outside and she began pointing northward and told me that "The Pearl" was the other cemetery in Reykjavik located up on a hill above the city. She sensed that I could not quite understand, so she directed me to a map of the city which is located just in front of the entrance to the cemetery, and we looked at it together.

At that moment we were standing very close together and then we sort of gazed into each other's eyes. It was one of those very brief moments that can, sometimes, last a lifetime. What happened next really illustrates why I am not yet married. For I felt like I was taking up too much of her time, which she had generously given to me, so I just thanked her for all her help and said "Bless" (The Icelandic "farewell").

How I could say goodbye without even asking her what her name was? As I walked away, I could only think, oh what a fool I am! But, then again, it was a Wednesday, and I would be free much of the next Wednesday, too, the last day of the trip, so I thought maybe I could go by and thank her again for all of her help and bring her a little gift. By then I should be able to inform her that I had found and visited the grave we had been searching for just before I asked her for her name and phone number or address so we could stay in touch with one another.

One of the things you hear about Icelandic women is how beautiful they are. This is without doubt true. Icelandic women are the most attractive in the world. They are not just all blondes either. You see many Icelandic women with dark, almost Middle Eastern, features who bring to mind the great Old Testament heroines, like Ruth and Esther, and many others with the freckles and red hair of an Irish beauty.

Yet the beauty of Icelandic women goes far beyond purely physical features. Indeed, Icelandic women are so beautiful that many men who know of this sometime come here wishing to use them as objects for their own pleasure. But the Icelandic woman is a true feminist. She does not allow herself to be objectified because of a certain dignity and strength of character she has developed throughout the centuries spent dealing effectively with all the hardships and challenges that Icelandic society has faced through the course of its history.

For this land is a land of fire and ice in both in a literal and a figurative sense. For two, maybe three, months a year in the summertime, it is a paradise unlike any other place on earth. The climate is mild, and it is light outside round the clock and the wonder and beauty of the Icelandic countryside is beyond description for even the finest writer (much less myself). But come winter and it is dark and cold and, historically, many of the men have had to work long hours away from home.

So, the women of Iceland have always been called upon to hold the homeland together through every challenge, and the beauty and purity of Icelandic culture and society is evidence of their great success. What a lesson the rather sad feminists of the United States could learn from the strength, dignity, and beauty of the Icelandic women. For while the United States feminists seek power by trying to be, look, and act like men, the Icelandic feminists reject this oxymoron, of being unfeminine feminists, and instead seek out the true strength, dignity, and beauty of the feminine and show it off like no other women, much less the unfeminine feminists of the United States. How great and powerful is the true feminism of the Icelandic women!

That true feminism of the Icelandic women is what I saw in the young woman of the cemetery. She was one of many young women out working to help keep Icelandic culture strong. She was honoring her culture's past through caring for the resting place of her ancestors. And she was prepared to be of total service to me as I sought to honor the memory of my Grandpa Willy. I hope that, even if I never meet her again, I might honor her in the way I conduct myself among those who truly honor and love their culture.

After having met "the young woman who honors her past," I walked back to the car and headed for Cousin Gully's house. Gully and her husband Runar and their family live just south of *Reykjavik*. After looking in a store for more gifts to bring them, because I was a little early, I arrived at their house just before 6:00 p.m.

Gully had sounded very much like her sister Birna on the phone, but she was actually shorter. Birna is very tall, and when she has babies she has girls, four of them, while Gully has four boys. They are both alike in being warm and welcoming people who are strong yet understanding. Gully was taking care of her grandson Kristofer (my father's name), who was just about to turn one year old. We talked about the family and about how Imba had taken care of her second Christopher, my sister Linda's son, years after having taken care of "Bubby."

After a while, Kristofer's mother arrived back from work to pick him up. Gully's oldest son, Runar, had married one of Iceland's most beautiful women who was very understanding and loving toward her little son even as he kept setting off his talking robot toy, over and over again, as his mother tried to make a phone call.

Gully's house was very nice, yet it was also comfortably informal. Her husband Runar had come from the largest town in the Westfjords of Iceland named *Isafjorour*. It is an enchanting little fishing village that literally looks as if it floats out upon the fjord. Runar is a very hard working and unassuming man, and, in that way, he reminded me of Daddy. His English was much better than my Icelandic, but we still could not communicate very well with words. Gully's English is very good as is her 17-year-old son Oscar's.

As we ate our dinner of salmon with baked potatoes, I told Gully that the most wonderful words I could have heard when I talked to her earlier that day were "come on over for a nice home cooked meal." She even burned the potatoes a little bit just the way I like them. I told her that the last memorable meal I had involving salmon was the time I had lunch with the Bishop of San Jose, along with some others, a few years before. I could tell she was impressed by that, yet I had only said it in order to make conversation.

After dinner we headed for Haddi and Palina's place. They live in a nice little retirement apartment just west of Gully. Aunt Palina reminds me very much of Aunt Bara in how she looks and in how she is very kind and reserved.

She greeted me affectionately and then thanked me for the chocolates I gave her. Uncle Haddi had been quite sick last year but was healthy now. He had the look of a man of legend. I could very easily imagine him as a Viking Chieftain who you would really not wish to see the bad side of. Yet Uncle Haddi is one of those rare people of whom nobody has anything bad to say. We greeted one another very affectionately with a hug.

It was very special for me to see my Great Uncle Haddi. He reminded me so much of Dad in his strong masculine presence. But my Great Uncle Haddi is also like Dad in how he loves to laugh and be independent. He walked with a cane, yet he would not let himself be treated in a special way. When he was a young man, he was a gymnast and he showed me a picture of himself doing a handstand on top of a stone block that was already several feet off of the ground. My Great Uncle Haddi was a strong man!

After a while, my cousin Kristen, Haddi and Palina's daughter, came by. She is tall and blonde like my sisters, yet she reminded me the most of

Aunt Swan in how she is very outgoing and fun to be around. She made me feel very welcome and at home. It was as if we had known each other our whole lives but just happened to meet for the first time that evening.

    We all talked for several hours about the family, and I showed around the family picture, of Mom and all of my brothers and sisters and I (taken just before Dad died). I also showed the picture of Dad at a company picnic, sitting on a park bench with his accordion in hand. When Great Uncle Haddi saw it, he let out a great laugh and cried out, "That are Bubby!" Aunt Palina is already planning a big "Kaffi" get together for when I come back around the island on the twelfth. She says it will be a big party, so I better be ready.

    After Gully and I left, she drove me straight to Grandpa Willy's cemetery. Haddi had told her where it was, but it was very late, and we were not exactly sure where his grave was, so we did not go inside. However, Gully promised me that she would find the grave of Grandpa and Uncle

Vilhelm by the time I came back around the island. Talking with Gully was fun because, although she was serious and respectful about the important things in life, she had a sort of mischievous and fun side of her personality as well.

At one point, Gully asked me why I had never gotten married, I told her that if I had lived in Iceland I would most certainly be married because Icelandic women are so beautiful [I am not single because I do not know how to say charming things]. We talked for quite a while after we got back to her house. I learned so many things about our family, not just who we are but how we are, talking to Gully that night.

After we said goodbye, I set off for the long drive toward my first farmhouse accommodation. You can easily talk all night in Iceland in the summertime because 10:30 pm seems like 7:00 pm in California. I arrived at the farmhouse just past midnight after a one-hour drive. The good dinner my cousin Gully had fed me had my cold feeling much better. She had really taken Grandma's place in looking after me in this simple way. Imba's spirit lives on in my Cousin Gully.

As I pulled into the *Efribru* farmhouse, just past midnight, it was still light outside and I could see and hear people sitting around inside singing Icelandic folk songs. The charm of it all was so uplifting. I honestly did not think that people sat around singing folk songs, something I love to do, anymore. I got my first good night's sleep while in Iceland that night and had, among other things, klaners (twisted up Icelandic doughnuts) with kaffi for breakfast the following morning.

A PILGRIMAGE TO ICELAND

CHAPTER SIX

THE GOLDEN CIRCLE

The "Golden Circle" is the most popular tourist attraction in Iceland. It consists of the *Alþingi*, *Geysir*, and *Gullfoss*. I had no doubt that the site of the *Alþingi* on the *Þingveller* plain was my first destination. It was the original site of the longest continuing democratic assembly in the world, The *Alþingi*.

The *Alþingi* began in 974 AD as an annual meeting of several Viking Chieftains in order to set laws, settle legal cases, and form new alliances. In 1000 AD, the *Alþingi* voted that Christianity would become the official religion of Iceland. My most prominent ancestor, Snorri Sturluson, had served two separate terms as the "Law Speaker" of the *Alþingi*. This was the most sacred and important political position in Iceland, for the Law Speaker was at the head of the *Alþingi*.

Once I arrived, I headed right for the "Law Speaker's Rock." I used the timer delay on my new camera, so I was in practically every photograph I took. I got one of me "speaking the law" on the "Lawgiver's Rock" just like Uncle Snorri used to do. At first, I was almost the only person there. Later, many German tourists arrived to investigating their own cultural history. I said hello to so many people.

I do not think it is really possible to describe what it was like to be at the *Alþingi*. I would imagine that I was walking about, gathered with my people, a thousand years ago. The *Alþingi* is truly a holy place of pilgrimage. What a son or daughter of Iceland encounters there is only for him or her to truly know. It is a new/old place one finds in their soul. I can only say that I now know what it means to be a part of the "line of my people" in a very deep, really phenomenological, sense. The *Alþingi* has changed my heart.

I was not as excited about seeing *Geysir* as I was about seeing *Gullfoss*. However, *Geysir* is right on the way to *Gullfoss*, so I thought that stopping by would do no harm. And all of the sulfur in the air was great for my cold! The actual *Geysir* has been rather quiet of late, but its little sister "*Strokker*" still puts on a fine show. I stayed behind the ropes, which are in place to keep people from getting soaked by the hot water, as I waited, camera in hand, but when it went off, I got soaked anyhow. Yet the water that fell upon me was not really all that hot, so I took it as being a sort of special Icelandic baptism.

The really memorable part of my visit there happened when I went into the gift shop afterwards in order to buy some little gifts to bring back home. Just as I was getting ready to pay, this blonde young lady who worked there, who looked like a true daughter of Iceland, smiled at me as I headed for the counter, so I went to her. I made some small talk as she checked out my stuff and at one point said: "My father was from Iceland, and I am the first of his children to visit here." Well, this daughter of Iceland just looked me right in the face and said, "That is sad." I just love the Icelandic habit of telling the truth bluntly.

I was full of excitement and anticipation over seeing *Gullfoss*. I had seen Grandma's painting of it since I was a child, and it hangs on my living room wall today. Well, it does not disappoint in person, and I took many pictures. I kept trying to get a picture of it from the same angle as Grandma's painting, but it was not possible. To get the perspective Grandma had, one would have to be suspended in the air above the river *Hvítá*. I am not quite sure how Grandma got that perspective while painting, but I know very well that when my Grandma Imba applied her will to a given task, that task was definitely going to get done.

She was not alone among Icelandic women in this. For at the foot of the falls, there is a stone plaque with a sculpture of Sigridur Tomasdottir on it. She is like the patron saint of the beauty, strength, and nobility of the Icelandic women. At one point, on no less than the orders of the King of Iceland and Denmark, a hydroelectric company had planned to dam up the river and thus destroy the falls. But when Sigridur heard of this she walked all the way to Reykjavik, at least a two hour's drive (she walked!) and told the government officials that if they did not stop all of this madness and save the falls, she would throw herself into them! Well, the government had a change of heart and has now preserved the falls for good. After all, what match is a hydroelectric company, a government bureaucracy, or even a King for a true daughter of Iceland like Sigridur Tomasdottir? (Who, unlike her namesake in John 20:24-27, had absolutely no doubt about what she believed in).

    I drove through southwest Iceland, between *Selfoss* and *Vik*, on the Ring Road to get to my lodging for the night. This area is the most beautiful I have ever seen. The *Seljalandsfoss* waterfall is, no doubt, the highlight of the ride as the elegant drop of the thin stream of water off a sheer cliff can be seen for miles down the Ring Road and is at its most beautiful close up. I got a wonderful picture of it with a rainbow running across the bottom.

Late in my ride, just before *Vik*, I drove past *Brekkur* farm. It is where my Great Grandma Guajawia (sounds like "Virginia") came from. Tomorrow I will make a visit there. I feel very at peace with this land of Great Grandma Guajawia and my other ancestors. It is deep in my soul.

I had the most wonderful dinner of Halibut with white wine at my farmhouse tonight. I felt so satisfied that I just sort of sat there at my table in bliss for a long time. The young man who runs the farmhouse is named Borg. We had a nice conversation before dinner. He is not even my age yet has a beautiful Icelandic wife and daughter. He is a very blessed man. It made me think about what my life might have been like if I had always been here in Iceland.

CHAPTER SEVEN
THE MYSTERY OF FATHERHOOD

My head cold has come back with a fury in the night however whatever gloomy skies are in my physical body are countered by an absolutely beautiful day with bright sun, soft wind, and some majestic clouds floating gentle by. Right now, I am at *Kirkjubæjarklaustur* putting on some suntan lotion. Yet one can apparently get burned in *Kirkjubæjarklaustur* by more than just the sun.

For this is the site of the oldest settlement of Irish monks in Iceland. Some say they date back to the pre-Norse period and Saint Brendan's quest for the "Isle of the Blessed." Yet as any good theology student can tell you blessings are great, yet they also imply the existence of curses. And when the Vikings finally did come and force these Irish monks out it is said that they did indeed put a curse upon this place so that nobody who worshiped the Norse gods could live here. A man named "Ketill", whom the other Vikings called "foolish" for believing in Christ, lived here just fine after the monks left yet when a man named "Hildir", who still believed in the Norse gods, came to live here afterwards he dropped dead on the spot! It made the other Vikings wonder if Ketill was really so foolish for believing in Christ? Oh, how wonderful to be a fool for Christ!

Earlier this morning I was at the black sand beach at *Vik*. It is perhaps the most beautiful non-tropical beach in the world and out in the water these huge eerie looking stone figures stand as if they are keeping guard.

Vik is only 4-5 miles away from *Brekkur* farm where Great Grandmother Guajawia came from. When I got up the hill to the farm, I was amazed at the beautiful views of the valley below and the sea beyond it, the *Mydalsjokull* glacier to the northeast, and the beautiful pastoral scenes all around.

After looking around for a while, I finally got up the nerve to walk up to the nearest house and knock on the door. A tall blonde teenage boy, who did not look much unlike myself at that age, answered. I asked him if he spoke English and he nodded in approval. Next, I asked if this was actually *Brekkur* farm and he said "yes." So I told him that my Great Grandmother Guajowia had come from here and asked him his name. He said English speaking people could generally not pronounce it yet, after he sized me up a bit, he gave it a try anyhow. He told me his name was "Ickfuss" (phonetic pronunciation). I repeated it back to him and he was so surprised that I could pronounce it correctly that I said it again just to make a good impression. I started to engage him in some small talk about relatives, but he grew bored, as teenagers often do at such talk, and then offered for me to look around the farm at my leisure. I said, "Thank you, Ickfuss", and said farewell. The farm was rather ordinary looking in and of itself, but the surrounding views were incredible. I imagined Great Grandmother Guajowia looking out over these same views, years ago, wondering about her future life and where it might take her. Now here I was, a part of that future she must have imagined, looking out upon the same long unchanged landscape.

On my way back to *Vik*, I thought of her riding along with her family on a horse and buggy in order to attend Sunday services at the beautiful little *Vik* chapel that overlooks the town. The spire of the chapel being the first thing one notices after climbing the steep hill that lies at the very end of the trip between the farm and *Vik*.

What a symbol this climb must have been for Great Grandmother Guajowia! A symbol of how the holy and beautiful things in life are reached only through the struggle of the steep ascent. Yet, once that effort has been made, they flow to you naturally just like gravity propels you down that hill into *Vik* after you have reached the summit. What a very good lesson to learn from the land.

I am sitting down to dinner now after three cups of tea and a long afternoon nap. This little farmhouse cafe has an excellent view of the largest glacier in Europe, *Vatnajokull*, seemingly flowing down toward it through a pass in the foothills only a short distance away. With such a perilous scene as a constant reminded of creation's power, it is no wonder that the *Brunnhóll* farmhouse features its own little chapel adjoining the farm.

    I was talking with a nice Dutch couple who sat at the same table as I during dinner. Afterwards, we went to visit this same chapel which adjoins the farm. It measures about 30' X 15' and has a spire with a cross affixed to it outside. Inside, it has a vestibule, with a stairway leading to the choir loft, and a really beautiful interior featuring a hand carved Lectern and Baptismal Font. Yet the painting behind the altar is by far the highlight of it all.

    It is a painting of the Presentation (Luke 2:22) with the baby Jesus in the centre, looking almost like an airy Cherubim, with Simeon on his right and Mary on his left. They each have a hand on the baby Jesus, to show how they are supposedly holding him up, yet it is obvious that the baby Jesus does not need their support because he seems to be almost dancing in joy at the prophecy of Simeon.

> *Now, Master, you may let your servant go in peace, according to your word, for my eyes have seen*

> *your salvation, which you prepared in sight of all the peoples, a light for revelation to the Gentiles, and glory for your people Israel"* (Luke 2:29-32).

This is, of course, all wonderful and danceable material so far. Yet the next words from the Prophet's mouth seem much more stark and troubling:

> *Behold, this child is destined for the fall and rise of many in Israel, and to be a sign that will be contradicted [rejected] (and you yourself a sword will pierce) [He now says to Mary] so that the thoughts of many hearts will be revealed* (Luke 2:34-35).

The critical question one must ask about this painting is what exact moment in Simeon's prophecy is it attempting to capture? I believe that how one answer this question will do nothing less than display if that person understands the message of Christ. For those who believe Christ is dancing between Mary and Simeon only at the moment of being spoken of as the "glory of Israel" and not at the moment of being spoken of as "a sign that will be contradicted" do not know

Christ crucified! For any person will dance at the song of their own self-glory, yet only Christ, and those who know him, will dance at the song of their own self-offering. This is the critical distinction.

Yet there is another figure watching in the background of this painting. It is Joseph who intently watches the drama unfold yet does not become, outwardly, enmeshed within it. How can we understand his mysterious figure? Is he in the background because he is simply unimportant to the drama, or does his character actually hold the key to understanding the whole event?

My favorite picture of my father is one taken when I was a boy and our family was on a visit to Lake Tahoe. I had been dressed up in a red cowboy hat with a six gun (six cap gun) on my hip for much of the trip. My Uncle John and Aunt Margaret owned a couple of horses they let us ride and one of them was named "Thunder" or "Lightning" or some such thing, and it deserved the name.

Well, somebody decided that they wanted to get a picture of little cowboy Johnny on the horse, but I was terrified of the animal and did not wish to go anywhere near it. However, at one point I found myself placed on the back of this huge wild beast thinking, "No one can help me now if this horse bolts." I can remember holding on tight as the pictures were taken and being so very happy to get off the back of that horse! For a long time afterwards, I remembered that moment as a time of being in great danger and totally without help.

But then, years later, my mother gave me a copy of the picture and just behind me, in the background, was Daddy, intently watching over me should the horse decide to bolt. He had been protecting me all along, yet he never spoke of it or sought attention for it in any way. He was simply focused on my safety and my concerns above anything else.

That is the key to understanding the character of Joseph in the painting of the Presentation. He has so focused himself on Jesus and Mary that he himself has faded into the background almost completely. Yet the very near completeness of his disappearance is a direct sign of the very near completeness of his self-offering for his Wife and Son. Thus, the great mystery of Fatherhood is part of the great mystery of the Cross. For, whereas, before becoming the foster father of the Christ child, Joseph had been somewhat self-centred about his name and personal honor, like when he sought to quietly distance himself from Mary upon learning of her pregnancy, something about now fulfilling the office of Father has radically changed him. If only more fathers today would follow Joseph, in becoming focused on Jesus and Mary and hidden within the Cross, the great crisis of modern family life would surely fade away.

    Earlier today I visited *Skaftafell* National Park where I went on a nice hike up to the *Svartifoss* waterfall. When I finally reached it, I found myself in a situation where I really wanted to take a picture of myself, standing in front of the falls, but I simply had no place to put the camera. So, I asked a nice older man, who was there with another man, if he would take the picture for me and he did. As we hiked back down the hill, I began talking with him and several members of his family who were on the hike with him. The entire family had come to Iceland because this man's mother was a full-blooded Icelander who had never seen her homeland. But even more interesting than this for me was that she had always wanted to make the trip to Iceland with her husband, but he had died two years earlier before they ever got the chance. Suddenly I understood why God had brought me together with these nice people on the hike. I told them of my own motivations in coming to Iceland, about how my father and I had made similar plans, but I had lost him two years ago. This family had also made contact with many of their relatives and was planning to have a large reunion on June 17, Icelandic Independence Day, at the site of the *Alþingi* where I had visited only the day before. It is very good to know that others are on pilgrimage as well!

A father watching over his son.

CHAPTER EIGHT
A TALK WITH HARRY

    I am sitting at a picnic table next to a river which is supposed to contain a local monster within it. Since Iceland is rather an enchanted land, one is wise to give credence to such stories. So, I have decided to not sit with my back toward the river and to leave my cross necklace outside of my shirt. Caution, born out of a respect for local culture, is always advisable in such situations.

    It has been a gorgeous day for weather, but somewhat of a frustrating day for travel. This morning, after I got about a half hour away from my farmhouse, I discovered that I had forgotten to turn in the key for my room. I was really too far away to turn back, and I figured that they must have an extra key anyhow, yet I still felt bad that I might inconvenience them. The drive to *Egilsstadir* was beautiful. I decided to cut off the coastal route and take the shorter way in on the Ring Road. This was a good decision.

    The best, or first best, part of my trip occurred

just as I arrived in town and stopped at the Esso station. A teenage girl started pumping the gas for me, so I strolled inside, credit card in hand, in order to pay. I looked at the pretty redheaded girl behind the counter and, without saying a word, smiled and handed her my credit card. She was about to speak to me, but just before she did, she looked at the credit card and smiled and said, "I thought you were Icelandic." I told her that I had been having that trouble quite often and really needed to learn how to speak Icelandic soon.

After that I went looking for Iceland's only real old growth forest, but I drove down the wrong side of the fjord. So, there I was down the fjord on the wrong side, I think it is sort of like being up the river without a paddle, yet I ended up having an excellent view of the forest, so I snapped a couple of pictures and went to walk in it later.

After I got back to town, I decided to go talk to the nice girl at the Esso station again because I was having trouble finding the post office. I actually ended up talking to a young man behind the counter first, but then the nice young lady wanted to help me too, so we all ended up talking. I found out where the post office was but it is closed on Saturdays so I will have to wait until Monday to mail that key back to the Brunnhóll farmhouse.

Given this fact, I thought it would be a nice thing to call them and let them know, but the phone booth outside of the post office was locked. With all of these frustrations beginning to get on my nerves, I decided that it would be a good idea to just try to do something simple, like visiting the local museum. The local museum was not really the place to be with it being such a warm and sunny day outside so the receptionists and I were the only ones around. After I paid my *300 Kroners* entrance fee, the receptionist, "Lara", offered to become my own private museum guide as well.

The museum was actually quite interesting, it even had a very well preserved recently discovered Viking grave, and Lara was a very good museum guide. After the tour, I asked her if I could take a picture of her and, even though she was a bit embarrassed, she smiled and said yes. For me, being treated with such respect and kindness made the frustrations of the day seem far away. Yet what a tough day it could have been if not for the Esso girl and Lara, two teenage girls from *Egilsstadir* who brightened my day.

    I just finished actually walking through the forest, not just taking pictures of it from across the river, and I am struck by the Icelandic sense of informality. The forest is an important national park, yet there was no entrance fee, no parking lot, and no rangers breathing down your neck about every little thing you do. People in this culture just don't hassle other people about all of these stupid things all of the time. They just let you live your own life and expect that you will be responsible and respectful. I think it is great! I could get comfortable with Icelandic informality very easily. *Akureyri* tomorrow! I leave early.

    A gorgeous chambermaid just showed me to my room, and I was nearly struck down by her charm! She offered to carry one my bags on the way up. If she had been an American woman, I would have refused but since she is a beautiful and strong Icelandic woman I just gave it to her and said "thank you."

My room is on the third floor, with a view overlooking the town, and it is indescribably charming. This place is like a nineteenth century country hotel. "Fawlty Towers?" Not quite. It is more like that Chateau where they have the crazy chase scene in the end of "What's New Pussycat?" I am going to have to dress up nice for dinner tonight as it will be held in the charming old dining room downstairs.

It is 10:00 pm and I am writing this journal entry by the light from my window. I have a charming little desk lamp, yet none is needed. As a matter of fact, the illuminating pen which I am writing this journal with has not been utilized either. It has a built-in light, for writing in bed at night, but in Iceland in the summertime, darkness is nowhere to be found.

I had an excellent dinner in the hotel dining room consisting of lamb, potatoes, salad, and about five cups of tea. The dessert was a wonderful light cake filled with cream, which had various sweet fruits scattered throughout it. Sensing the occasion of eating in such a charming county inn dining room, I wore my best outfit composed of an off-white turtleneck, tanned pants, and a dark brown patterned sports coat—my "Professor look."

After dinner, I was engaged in conversation by a 75-year-old Danish man named "Harry." After having been charmed by the beauty, kindness, and warmth of the Icelandic women all day long it was actually quite nice to engage in some conversation with another man, especially an older gentleman, for a change of pace if nothing else.

Harry is an existentialist who believes that man created God rather than that God created man. Despite my intellectual contempt for his ideas, I did my best to talk with him in a very respectful manner. Harry asked me if I was a philosopher and attempted to make that determination based upon the facts I knew rather than on how I thought. After all, it is one thing to have read all of the works of Kierkegaard and Nietzsche, yet quite another to be able to discern the fruits that such a reading might bring.

Harry troubled me because he insisted on not letting the conversation flow on, what he perceived to be, my narrow terms. Yet he simply replaced one set of "perceived" narrow terms with his own set of, actual, narrow terms, that existence precedes essence, taken right out of the existentialist credo. I tried to get Harry to realize that the entire premise of his way of thinking needed to be the subject of our conversation instead of the, rather secondary, conclusions which flow from it.

The ironic thing about the whole situation is that Jean Paul Sarte, the founder of modern existentialism, complained about exactly the same thing when he said (paraphrasing) that if one is authentically considering suicide, the very act of consulting a Catholic priest about it robs the choice of its authenticity because any Catholic priest would always advise against suicide (at least Sarte had an admirable confidence in the priesthood). Yet, now, Harry the existentialist has robbed himself of the very ability to make free and authentic choices, that his tradition supposedly so highly values, by turning his philosophy into his dogma. What a sad state the philosophy of the twentieth century must have been in to have led Harry on such an, ironically, useless chase for meaning in life.

However, I believe that the fact that Harry sought to engage me in conversation on these issues is a sign that he realizes the inability of his personal philosophy to satisfy and is, thus, opened to something more. I hope that by being willing to openly engage Harry in conversation, while treating him with the dignity and respect due to all persons, his heart and mind might begin to become more open to the greater possibility of a life with inherent meaning that a person who realizes that he is a creation of God enjoys.

A PILGRIMAGE TO ICELAND

A PILGRIMAGE TO ICELAND

CHAPTER NINE

ACCEPTING THE INVITATION

As I left town this morning, they played "To All the Girls I've Loved Before" on the car radio. I laughed and laughed thinking of all of the charming girls I met in *Egilsstadir*. When I went with Dad to Texas, the driveway of his little ranch was in bad shape, but he just had a friend of his throw some gravel on it. Well, in driving down the Ring Road, I have come to find exactly where he learned that method from.

I was thinking about how surprised some of the people at the farmhouses have been when they learned I am traveling alone. Yet being up here in the desolate eastern highlands, without even any sheep around, I feel the presence of divine providence enveloping my person. I am never alone because God is within me through my Baptism and all around me through His creation. What a great grace it is to occasionally realize that fact.

I have now stopped at *Goðafoss* (The Waterfall of the gods). It is only about 50 kilometers from Akureyri and can be seen from some distance up on the hill the Ring Road comes down. It is definitely better to travel around Iceland counterclockwise in order to get the dramatic long-distance effect of both *Seliajandsfoss* and *Goðafoss*. You could practically drive right past them without even realizing it if you were coming around clockwise.

Goðafoss itself is surreal. It is not as large as I imagined, only 12 meters high, but the effect one feels when peering down the throat of the river *Skjálfandafljót* at it makes it seem ten times larger. Part of it must be actually seeing it for the first time. I have seen so many of these sights in Grandma's paintings since I was a little boy yet, now, to actually see them come to life has brought me a great revelatory joy! I was thinking about Grandma as I sat on the cliff gazing at *Goðafoss*. I imagined how she must have looked and where she must have stood while painting it. Were not her paintings an invitation to her loved ones of how beautiful her homeland is and how we should all try to see it one day? I feel her presence as a great peace in my soul being here. I have accepted the invitation!

Goðafoss has its own tale to tell. When I was a boy and saw Grandma's painting and how spectacular this waterfall looks, I always assumed when I heard its name that it had something to do with how the gods would wish to show honor to such a beautiful thing. Yet it turns out that *Goðafoss* got its name in a way I did not originally expect.

It is said that after the *Alþingi* meeting of the year 1000AD, in which Iceland as a whole accepted Christianity, a Chieftain who lived out this way in the East was on his way back home. As he traveled and considered the implications of having accepted the new Christian faith, he was inspired to perform the act of throwing all of his idols that represented the Norse gods into this waterfall. He was inspired to literally perform an "act of faith."

The implications of this act toward

understanding Christianity in Iceland should not be passed over. For an Icelander, to follow Christ is not to talk but to act. To engage yourself into some sort of a real tangible action where your faith in Christ is displayed. It is no wonder that the "faith alone" message of the Reformation was not popular in Iceland and that the Icelanders were only willing to give up their Catholic faith at the point of a sword. I have a hunch that although they "officially" gave up their Catholic faith in 1550 AD, and were thus the last place in Europe to do so, unofficially it has survived to this day.

I have finally arrived in *Akureyri* and today is Sailor's Day. Right now, I am sitting on the dock listening to music. Many young families are here, and many young children are sitting on shoulders rising above the crowd. Icelandic people celebrate with great joy. Two men were on stage earlier doing an impression of Eminem. They later sang "The Monkey Song" in Icelandic. One of them reminded me of Dad and the great fun he would have when he entertained us with his accordion.

He learned how to play by ear and was quite good. As a boy, I was amazed just at the fact that he could lift up his huge accordion, none the less play it so well. He would play joyful Polkas, yet he would also play very heartfelt slower songs. He was a true artist in that he would become totally absorbed by the music and the huge accordion would become like a part of his body. I think it was the heart.

Some of the old sailors were on stage earlier receiving awards. I wonder if Grandpa Willy or Daddy ever sailed with any of them? The lady leading the singing now reminds me so much of Aunt Swan and how she would dance about at family gatherings full of life and joy. It is so strange to think that she and Erla and Daddy were all kids at this celebration sometime in the 1930's.

I took the ride out to *Dettifoss* this afternoon after very much enjoying *Akureyri*. The net result is that I drove for 5 hours, and am now very tired, but I did see *Dettifoss* and took some great pictures. I am going to have so much fun when I get back figuring out which one of Grandma's paintings is of which waterfall. Now I am the expert.

    Right now, I am sitting in my room at the *Rauoaskrioa* farmhouse, north of *Akureyri*, and the sun is shining brightly on the wall in front of my little desk. That is not so unusual except for the fact that it is 10:00 pm and that no part of the sun has touched the hill which it is setting over yet. There are a group of Icelandic horses grazing in a green meadow framed by my window. The scene in my window looks better than most paintings, and has the added benefit of being real.

    Earlier today, I saw the old family house in Akureyri which Aunt Swan had told me about and sent a picture of. There is much to tell of it. However, I intend to be asleep before the sun hits that hill so that tale will have to wait for another day.

Dettifoss.

CHAPTER TEN
CHRIST IS PRESENT IN AKUREYRI

I have come back to *Akureyri* this morning and we are having the first non-spectacular day for weather since that first day in Reykjavik when the wind was so cold that it hurt my ears. I actually took care of two items of business this morning as I got some pictures copied, to give to my relatives, and went to the post office and mailed that key back to the *Brunnhóll* farmhouse.

I am in the Botanical Gardens now, and many young people are here working to get the place in top shape for the summer (just as they were in Reykjavik). I can imagine Grandma kneeling over a plant, taking great care in her gardening work, all those years ago. [It turned out that Aunt Swan and Aunt Erla had actually worked in this garden as children for the wage of getting to keep their gardening shovels!].

This neighborhood here in *Akureyri* is like a dream. You have a house on the side of the hill with a great view and an empty lot across the street, with an even better view, for the children to play in. Then, about 100 meters up the road, you have this beautiful Botanical Gardens and, just above the house up the hill, you also have a hospital. The great Lutheran Cathedral is but a quarter mile away and the beautiful old house that is *Akureyri's* only Catholic Church is closer still (only about 100 meters from this garden). Just below the great Lutheran Cathedral is the downtown shopping district with the docks, where the Sailor's Day festivities were held, just beyond. Grandpa Willy could have walked home from them (and as it turns out he often did).

The *Akureyri* Botanical Gardens, which I am sitting in, was set up by a local women's organization in 1912 and was run by them, mostly with female volunteers, until the city took it over in 1950. Dad's family lived here from about the early 1930's to the late 1930's, so Grandma was, most likely, one of the women who volunteered here because her house, at Splitvager #9, was only about 100 meters away. The *Akureyri* Botanical Gardens are now world famous, and very nice to be in, even early in the season, and contain over 2000 species of blooming flowers. So perhaps we can add a fraction of one more accomplishment to Grandma's (and Swan and Erla's) legacy.

As I walk down into town the wind has come up so I have decided to buy an Icelandic sweater. Not as a tourist's prize but, instead, for very practical reasons.

I just bought my Icelandic sweater from a lady who was so much like Grandma. I went into the shop, out on the docks, and tried on a brown sweater. I was about to buy it, because I like them in brown, but the lady told me I could not buy one until I had tried on two or three of them because she did not like the way it fit me. I tried on another brown one but then she decided that brown was not the best color for me, so I tried on a black, gray, and white one which fit me perfectly. The lady approved of the fit and color of this sweater, so she let me buy it!

Ironically, it has the same exact coloring as the one Grandma had made for me, along with all of my brothers and sisters, when I was a boy. This woman had me so mesmerized with her presence and voice that I felt like a little boy saying "Yes Grandma" the whole time.

I am sitting in a little Icelandic Cafe on the pedestrian mall just across from the *Bokval* shop. This place is absolutely dripping with atmosphere from the custom fired plates with a scenic picture of *Akureyri* on them and the town's name in gold lettering, to the natural wood paneling and the crystal and silver chandeliers hanging over most of the tables. Due to the weather, this cafe is an even more popular spot today than usual and I recognize many of the people who have been staying at the same farmhouses as I in the crowd.

The slice of cake I ordered has a hard chocolate coating on top with a lighter, both in color and consistency, chocolate below, followed by whipped cream, followed by a wheat bread like crust. My Capuchin and cake cost *700 Kroners*, about $7, which is about what you would pay for something similar in the US. The handmade Icelandic sweater I bought cost 6900 Kroners, about $69, which is about $20 less than you would pay for the factory-made ones they sell in the tourist shops. I thought of buying one for my Mom but they fit each person so uniquely that one must really be here for a personal fitting.

I feel much more comfortable in town here today, having already gotten a "feel" for things yesterday. (Oh, there is some shortbread just below the light chocolate in the cake). The conclusion of the entertainment at yesterday's "Sailor's Day" was one of Iceland's "World's Strongest Men" coming up on stage and challenging several men from the crowd to perform acts of physical strength, like tearing a phone book in half, bending a steel spoon, and bending an iron bar. He then ridiculed them, all in Icelandic of course, when they failed. It was hilarious.

While all of this was going on, a long line was forming up the dock where many children were waiting in order to get a free ride on one of the beautiful new fishing boats in the Icelandic fleet. There were many very young children all about the dock and some of them would wander out near the edge, where I was sitting, which only had a very short wood border, perhaps a foot high, between it and the cold and deep waters of the fjord. I was constantly preparing myself to jump into these waters should any of these children slip over the edge. I was certainly not looking forward to getting the chance, but I figured it would either result in me becoming a real live Icelandic hero or a martyr who would be honored along with all of the other heroes on "Sailor's Day" for years to come. I just hoped, in either case, I would be able to pull the child out successfully.

There was one of the very old sailors on the dock yesterday who looked almost like Grandpa Willy's ghost! His eyes were tired like he had seen many things in life (perhaps too many). I very much doubted if he could speak English, so I did not attempt to talk to him. As a matter of fact, I did not see him go on stage to receive his medal, like the other sailors, of talk to anyone else. So perhaps it was Grandpa Willy come down to celebrate "Sailor's Day" one more time? I hope he knew one of his own line was there with him.

I have come back to the Botanical Gardens in the old neighborhood once again. I parked my car down near the Lutheran Cathedral because I just love to make the walk up and down the hill. Walking in my father's footsteps makes me very happy. The great beauty of this place and the intelligence of its arrangement makes it absolutely unforgettable. It is no wonder now why Grandma and Daddy always spoke of *Akureyri* with such fondness. This little town on a fjord up at the top of the world cannot be topped to the best of my knowledge.

From the almost terrifying ride over a high mountain pass, mostly without a guardrail, on the Ring Road that you must make to get here from the east to the beautiful view you get of the town from across the fjord as you approach it, the place makes itself simply unforgettable. It is another reason why one should always go around Iceland counterclockwise.

It is getting to be the time in the afternoon that I should be thinking of getting down the road. Yet I feel so at peace sitting in this garden that my Grandma and two Aunts helped nourish and my Father played in. I hope, perhaps, some of the longing which Grandma and Daddy felt for *Akureyri* and this wonderful neighborhood and garden has been lessened through my being here. I hope that they have somehow shared in the joy I have felt in being here in *Akureyri*.

The lady who sold me the sweater, who was so much like Grandma, said that I could find out about the things that are in my Father's soul by being here. I told her that I could not only do that but that I could make my own soul more complete, as well. That is what *Akureyri* has done for me. It has opened up a beautiful new place, which is ironically really a very old place, in my soul that I can share with Grandpa, Grandma, Swan, Erla, and Bubby. I hope that others in the family may one day come to *Akureyri* so they might enter into that sharing and, thus, open up a beautiful new/old place in their own souls, too.

As I leave this place, the sign that captures my attention the most is the spire on the Catholic church pointing toward the sky with the Cross atop it. This is done in church architecture in order to remind one of the greater things that await us above. Although being in *Akureyri* lessons the need for one to think of such things, the effect is still present.

Everywhere I go, the Catholic Church is present. For Dad, too, it was always present. The little Catholic church here in *Akureyri* is only about 200 meters from his boyhood home. Ironically enough, the Sacrament of Confession was the thing Dad disliked the most about the Catholic church, yet the actual Confessional here in the little church at *Akureyri* is one of the most beautiful I have ever seen.

Yet, of all the things that are so wonderful about the old neighborhood it is the continuous presence of Christ in the Blessed Sacrament within the Tabernacle of the little Catholic church, right in the heart of it all, which is by far the greatest. In no other place or neighborhood have

I seen the beauty of the Blessed Sacrament within so well reflected in all of the surroundings outside. Christ is present in *Akureyri!*

How good it makes me feel that Dad died being thought of as a Catholic. What a great mystery the Church must have been to him? Christ was present here in his boyhood home and then he traveled thousands of miles to the United States and married a Catholic woman. Being a man who respected divine providence, I think maybe he got the idea at some point before he died—perhaps when the Priest came to give him Last Rites, or maybe when his son prayed the Rosary over him in his hospital bed. "From ashes you have come and to ashes you shall return" (Ash Wednesday Liturgy). Somewhere in the place in-between, mostly during certain critical moments, you find out who you really are. The days are short—choose Christ!

I have arrived at my last farmhouse, *Staoarskali.* I ran into Harry and his wife heading for dinner, so we all ate together. Harry worked as a machinist, and he loves to sit around and tell stories. I also shared with him many stories about working with Dad in the machine shop and all of the fun and interesting times we had there. Every young boy should be so fortunate as to have worked with his father. Those are some of the best memories.

After dinner I went back to my room and called Gully. I was sorry to hear that she had caught the nasty cold I have been fighting, yet she was in good spirits in any case. The family gathering at Haddi and Palina's is on for tomorrow. I got enlargements of the family picture and the picture of Dad playing the accordion ("That are Bubby!") to give as gifts to the family. I also have some wine and whiskey left to give as gifts. I can hardly wait for it to start!

Tomorrow is going to be a family reunion day in another way, too, because I am going to visit our most famous ancestor's old farm at *Reykholt*. I do not know whether to call him "Uncle Snorri" or maybe just "Sir", but being at his place will be very special.

CHAPTER ELEVEN
THE FAMILIY GATHERING

    I'm driving down road 50 on the way to Uncle Snorri's place at *Reykholt*. This road is remarkably similar to the highway that leads into Hollister, the great difference being that there are sheep in the fields instead of crops. I can see why Dad loved to live in the Hollister of 20 years ago and was willing to make that long drive each day to work.

    The radio stations here in Iceland play better music than the ones at home. They are playing "My Old Flame" right now. It goes, "My old flame, I can't even think of her name, but every new fling I can only compare to my old flame." I guess that is how Daddy felt about Iceland. I can definitely understand why.

    I am just leaving *Reykholt* now. When I first arrived, the place appeared to be deserted, so I just took a little stroll around and said a prayer by the statue of Uncle Snorri. You can hardly miss the place as you approach it on the road because the new church's tower looks like it is a rocket that is about ready to get shot into orbit. The museum is actually located in the crypt of the new church, and it is a very wonderful place to visit and learn all about Uncle Snorri.

When I went in, the young lady behind the counter asked me if I was interested in Snorri and I told her that I was actually a far-flung descendant of his. She did not even bat an eye but just told me how I must be related to Snorri's father, a character in one of the Sagas, too. I guess the family must stop by often.

The thing I realized from being at *Reykholt* is that Snorri Sturluson was not just a Christian, but was actually a very well trained Catholic theologian who always made sure that there was a good priest on his estate and a fervent religious practice. How good it is to know that my most important Icelandic ancestor was a good Catholic who had studied theology and made the Church an important part of his life. I never realized all of the things that I hold in common with Uncle Snorri until today. He is my new friend in the family.

It is almost 1:00 am yet it is still perfectly light outside. I was driving in downtown *Reykjavik* on my way to the hotel, just past midnight, and all was light and the town was alive. I got lost and ended up out by the harbor, so I stopped and took a picture of the Viking Ship sculpture with Reykjavik Bay in the background. Nobody will guess that I took that picture at midnight.

I went to Gully's house at about 4:00 pm this afternoon. I saw her mom, Sigga, for the first time since I was a little boy, and she is looking well. Gully was still fighting her cold, so I promised I would give her some "medicine" for it later. Then we all headed over to Haddi and Palina's place.

The Icelandic *Kaffi* is a traditional family gathering where as many members of the family come together as possible and enjoy good company, excellent food, and, of course, *kaffi*. Great Aunt Palina had done a wonderful job in planning and preparing this gathering and because of that I got a chance to meet several more members of the family. And this is without even mentioning all the wonderful Icelandic treats, the likes of which I had not seen in many years, I got to eat, as well. [My Mother was to remark later, when looking at pictures of this gathering, that she had rarely seen such a happy smile from me as was on my face this day].

Kristen was there, along with her sister Valborg. Kristen had been to her first golf lesson that very day so I told her that the next time I came to Iceland, I would speak Icelandic if she would play golf with me. This sort of good-natured humor drew a large laugh from all present (whether they could speak English or not). Valborg did not speak much English, yet her smile and warmth as a person were capable of overcoming such barriers.

Two of my other cousins who are sisters were also present. My cousin Jona also brought along her beautiful daughter, Lisa. My other cousin, Inga, and I talked quite a bit. She works in a library, and I have been described as a natural born librarian, because of my love for books, so we had a natural understanding of one another.

Great Uncle Haddi gave me some wonderful old pictures of Grandpa Willy and Dad. Dad looks just like Jimmy Stewart in one of them. Grandpa Willy is in full uniform on a dock with a shipmate in the other. Great Uncle Haddi also showed me a picture of Aunt Swan, Aunt Erla, and Dad taken when Dad was about 16 years old. Aunt Swan and Aunt Erla look so beautiful and Dad so handsome that this picture looked like a professional modeling shot rather than a family portrait. Aunt Erla actually was a model around that time, and I believe Aunt Swan and Dad were only not models for a lack of trying.

I told everybody of my trip and the journal I had been keeping during it. It felt sort of awkward to be right in the middle of enjoying a family get together that everybody knew I was later going to be writing about, so I decided then and there to be very sensitive about privacy. This was certainly not due to any lack of openness or sharing on the part of my Icelandic relatives but more out of the deep appreciation and respect I had quickly gained for them all.

Runar and Gully had offered to take me out to the Blue Lagoon that evening, so everything broke up around 7:00 p.m. I tried to make the excuse for having to leave early that I needed to give Gully her "medicine," but Cousin Jona saw right through it. I find that you can really tell someone is a member of your family by how easily they can see through your little fibs. Dad used to look right through me like I was a magnifying glass.

Another reason that I wanted to get going was that Gully and I were planning to go by the cemetery and look for Grandpa Willy's grave later that evening. We headed to the *Hafnarfjorour* cemetery and began to look for the grave. Yet even after we had both searched and searched, we could not find it. Finally, Gully showed me where the caretakers office was, which was closed at that hour of the evening, and told me that she was sure that the caretaker would find the grave for me if I stopped by tomorrow.

Gully then took me to this place called the "Viking Village." It is a place where one can go live like a Viking for a while if one desires. The buildings which make it up are actually an old foundry. One of them is used as a restaurant and is a very impressive replica of an old Viking Hall, right down to the wooden plates. The other building is used as both a museum and a hotel. Gully asked me to wait a few minutes in the restaurant as she went and got something. The place was empty at that hour, yet the atmosphere made it easy to imagine Vakerie walking about serving and Vikings seated having a great feast. When Gully came back, she presented me with my first Viking drinking horn! I felt like I had just been named an eagle scout or something. Suddenly at that moment I knew I was truly an Icelander (and now I have a drinking horn to prove it!).

    When we got back to her house, I presented Gully with my own gift of American whiskey to serve as her cold medicine. She immediately poured some into a large drinking glass and drank it right down and said, "It's too sweet John!" Yet it did make her throat feel better. I had originally intended to give it as a gift when I first arrived but when my cold came on I decided to hold onto it for a while (as it has long been my cold medicine of choice).

When Runar got back from work, he took us all on a long drive out in the country and we ended up at the Blue Lagoon. The Blue Lagoon is actually located in the runoff area of a hydroelectric plant. It is a sort of testament to the resourcefulness of the Icelandic people because somebody discovered that the white mud in this water is very good for the skin, so now there is a clinic and major tourist attraction there. I got something nice for my brother Steven, in order to round out my family gifts, while there.

Runar took us by his cabinet making shop on the way back. My brother Richard is also a cabinet maker, so I told Runar and Gully that "this is what Richard does." Runar had one new machine of which he was particularly proud. At one point, I even pointed my camera at him to take a picture and he motioned for me to take a picture of the new machine instead. [Later, I showed this picture to Richard, and he was amazed that the latest cabinet making machine, which his shop did not even yet have, was already being used by Cousin Runar].

    Runar and Gully and I drank a toast with American whiskey after we got back. We did not actually say what the toast was to, but, instead, just said "Skoal." As I raised my glass with Runar, I realized that, since I had officially received my Horn, I was drinking my first toast with an Icelander as an Icelander. I was drinking to their hospitality, and they were drinking to Bubby's son, who had come to Iceland in his father's place and found his own place. Runar and Gully offered for me to stay with them the next time I come to Iceland. I can only hope that it will be soon.

CHAPTER TWELVE

HE GIVE GIFT!

Grandpa's grave says:

>Vilhelm FR. Jonsson
>Velstjori
>F.7.9.1897 D.4.9.1985
>Matth.5.3-11

Uncle Vilhelm's grave says:
>Vilhelm Vilhelmsson
>3.2.1934
>29.6.1934

The name of the woman Grandpa Willy lived with for many years is below his own on the relatively new looking gravestone. Grandpa's grave has a lantern on it. Uncle Vilhelm's has a simple maker stone with a cross at the top. The graves are located in section A-49 of the *Hafnarfjorour* cemetery. Although the route has now changed, at that time h you passed right by this cemetery, on your right, as you came into *Reykjavik* from the airport. It is up on the top of a hill.

I stopped and cleaned off the markers and left some flowers. I prayed the Rosary and chose the Glorious Mysteries. They speak of Jesus and Mary being united in heaven with God the Father. For me this speaks of all families being one day united.

I have stopped for a bite to eat now. I finally found that KFC I had been looking for. Iceland has the best KFCs on the planet! The food is very reasonably priced, and you get more than one person could possibly eat at a sitting. There is even no ice in the drinks.

Seeing the graves of Grandpa Willy and Uncle Vilhelm was very emotional for me. But I am not sad because I know we will one day be together. It is just that I felt so close and connected to them for the first time.

I only have only two hours left now before I must drive to the airport. Yet I have an appointment to keep in downtown Reykjavik at the old cemetery before I go. The man at the *Hafnarfjorour* cemetery was very helpful. He even ran me down in the cemetery after I initially started looking in the wrong section. Icelandic people seem to have a sense of the important, really sacred, things in life, like looking for the grave of a long lost loved one.

I guess I have accomplished everything Dad would have originally set out to do. It all seems to be wrapped up in a nice little package. Praise God for that! Yet I have one more thing to do just for myself now.

As I walk down into the heart of downtown Reykjavik, on the bridge over the *Tjornin*, I feel very happy inside. I have just seen "the young woman who honors her past" and given her the gifts I brought for her and her mother and father. I walked into the old cemetery, down the same path as before, hoping to see her. Although many young people were in sight, she or her mom or dad were nowhere to be seen. I even peeked into the little office where they had all helped me before but there was no sign of them.

But then, as I walked out of the office, I saw her giving instructions to a group of young people who were getting ready to work in the cemetery.

She was the woman in charge! Then, I walked up nearer to her until I caught her attention. I said "hello" and asked if she remembered me from last week. She said "yes" (I took this as a very good sign) and I told her that I had found my grandfather's grave in the *Hafnarfjorour* cemetery. She was surprised that I had found it there and not at the "Pearl." Next, I handed her the little bag with all the gifts inside and said, "I wanted to give you a gift for all of your help last week."

Her response was to smile at me and say, "Why?" through her thick Icelandic accent. I told her that it had been "my first kindness while in Iceland" (which maybe was not strictly true yet the only thing that came to mind at the moment). I then said "good-bye" and as I walked down the path, I heard her say to her friends and fellow workers; "He give gift!" in a sort of joyful and surprised tone.

Now I am sitting in the little park on the other side of the *Tjornin*, near the National Gallery, looking at a statue of a man and a woman embracing one another in a kiss. The woman seems much more active than the man in this kiss, what do you expect of an Icelandic woman, but from where I am at, I cannot see her face too well.

I guess it is still really that way with "the young woman who honors her past." I still don't know her name, or have her number, or know much any mundane knowledge about her at all. But I do know that I just made her very happy. And I know that knowing that makes me so very happy.

The statue of the man and the woman speaks so perfectly of romantic love because the man is kissing the woman, however, the woman is really kissing the man. He has captured her heart and now she is doing all she can to express her total self-donation toward him. That is why I did not try to get a picture or the name of "the young woman who honors her past." I want to be a mystery to her and allow her to be a mystery to me. If I ever do capture her heart, she will find me. She is an Icelandic woman—she will hunt me down!

This day is more glorious than all the others. The sun is bright, the wind is soft, and young people are all over town clipping and mowing and planting. It is as if they are all saying, "This is our town and we will make it beautiful." No doubt they will yet certainly, by their very presence, they already have.

As I took my one last walk through the streets of Reykjavik, I was thinking about how nobody has stopped me thinking I was someone else, as happens to me in the US quite often. Then, as I walked out of town for the final time on the bridge over the *Tjornin*, a young woman walked right by me who looked just like my old friend Elizabeth. I could not believe the resemblance to such an extent that I almost stopped her and asked, "What are you doing here?" Perhaps it is a sign that my old friend is praying for me.

As I was driving down Road 41 on my way to the airport, they were playing this absolutely surreal music box like dream sequence music on the radio. It must have stayed on for at least 20 minutes. I was just letting all of the beautiful memories of this trip gently flow through my mind. It was an epiphany—a moment of grace!

It brings my thoughts back to Simeon and how he must have felt when he said, "Now, Master, you may let your servant go in peace" (Luke 2:29). All has been accomplished. Some seeds have been brought to fruition while others have been planted. I did everything I could do and even stopped by the *Tjornin* on the way out of town and dropped off some extra bread I had by where they feed the ducks. The people sitting around there just sort of looked at me strangely as I held up the bread and said, "Food for the ducks" and left it lying near a bench. I kept on thinking about how Saint Francis would have approved.

As I sit around here in the airport terminal wearing my grungy old "Indiana Jones" hat, I think about what an adventure I have been on. I honored the memory of father by coming here when he had planned to. I met many wonderful relatives I had never met before and saw many others I had not seen since I was a small child. I drove all the way around this "Island at the Top of the World" and came to know the heart and the spirit of my people better through seeing how and where they live. And, finally, I did my best to woo "the young woman who honors her past" and made her very happy in the process.

The second song they played on the radio on the way over here asked, "Is this the beginning or is this the end?" Before I came to Iceland, many long worked for goals were either completed or came much closer into view. During the long process of bringing that all about, I had begun to feel very old and tired inside like I was at an end. Yet Iceland has made me see the possibility of a wonderful new beginning. It has given me a sense of wonder and hope about living that I have not really felt for a long time—certainly not since Dad died. Since going on this trip was really his last great gift to me, this sense of a new beginning is a part of Dad's gift. I hope that I will cherish this gift and bring it to fruition.

A PILGRIMAGE TO ICELAND

EPILOGUE

The Sacred Scripture on Grandpa Willy's gravestone is Matthew 5:3-11. It reads:

Blessed are the poor in spirit, for theirs is the kingdom of heaven.

Blessed are they who mourn, for they will be comforted.

Blessed are the meek, for they will inherit the land.

Blessed are they who hunger and thirst for righteousness, for they will be satisfied.

Blessed are the merciful, for they will be shown mercy.

Blessed are the clean of heart, for they will see God.

Blessed are the peacemakers, for they will be called children of God.

Blessed are they who are persecuted for the sake of righteousness, for theirs is the kingdom of heaven.

> *Blessed are you when they insult you and persecute you and utter every evil against you because of me.*

What strikes me the most about this particular citation of the Beatitudes, beyond its inherent beauty and truth, is that verse 12 (*Rejoice and be glad, for your reward is great in heaven*) is not included. Most citations of this passage include verse 12 because it really sums up the promise of reward one can expect for following the Beatitudes.

I sense a story here yet need time to reflect upon it. The connotation of the omission of verse 12 seems to be of a person being willing to suffer without any regard for the promises of glory that said suffering might bring. This is an act of incredible humility and bravery. Most people are not strong enough to even begin to attempt to live out the message of the Beatitudes without putting an emphasis on the blessings promised in the second part of each verse. For is it not simply human nature to seek blessing and glory when one does good? Perhaps not.

What Grandpa Willy's gravestone suggests is a radical faith in Christ which only a very brave, strong, and humble person would ever consider, much less take up. Yet, in my experience of the Icelandic Spirit, not only on this pilgrimage but also throughout my life within my family, I see the strength, humility, and bravery to live radically for Christ. Yet, this faith is much more about actions than words, and it shines through most brightly in a willingness to bravely and humbly suffer for others—especially other family members.

   I think of Grandma Imba, who worked tirelessly to help my mother and father in raising up all my brothers and sisters and I, and even some of her great grandchildren, their children, too. Her energy and efforts will forever be remembered not only as the finest example of the strength and humility of the Icelandic women, but as one of the finest examples of womanhood itself.

   My Aunt Bara (whose name means "little ripple of water"), who, by her delicate and caring heart, always welcomed me, as a little boy, to come and sit with her in her room and enjoy The Lawrence Welk Show's music and elegance as she shared with me the great meaning of much of the music for herself—especially "Stormy Weather."

My Dad, who worked tirelessly to provide "a roof over your head and food on the table" (as he loved to say) for his family while also being a very generous friend to many others, as well. And who, even after my parent's divorce, strove to help his children to grow up to be hard working and responsible people who always respected the dignity and freedom of others.

My Aunt Swan, who is full of a zest for life and has the wonderful Icelandic quality of telling the truth bluntly, yet always being more happy to tell of a noble truth than a fault. Her encouragement of my noble ideal for marriage, spoken at a family gathering years ago, lives on in me as I meditate on what the role of a good husband should be.

My Aunt Erla, who I have begun to grow closer to through the writing of this journal. In her I have discovered a fellow Catholic who has the sort of wisdom which can only come through the Cross, and a heart that is warm, generous, and strong. If coming to better know her is the only fruit of this journal, I will consider it a great success.

My Cousin Birna, who encouraged me because of the small act of nobility, done as a very young man one year at the Christmas party, of following her outside to be sure she was safe, after a strange man had knocked on the door and asked her to move her car, by saying, "You're a sweetheart." (I greatly enjoyed telling that story to her sister Gully while in Iceland).

And now I have a whole new part of the family in Iceland I have just discovered who have brought a whole new source of encouragement and good example into my life. Meeting them all has filled up an empty place in my heart!

Is there not a connection between the "Why" spoken by "the young woman who honors her past", after I gave her a gift, and the omission of verse 12? Are not both examples of a very natural and genuine belief in the Icelandic culture that good and noble deeds should be done simply because they are good and noble and not out of any expectation of reward?

As I come to the conclusion of this journal, I think back on the question I asked at the beginning of this pilgrimage. "How will better understanding myself through knowing the past help me to truly enter into communion with others?"

Being in Iceland was a revelation for me because, when I was in this strange place which I had never been in before, I felt a greater sense of family and community than I do while at home. I never realized what it is like to be a part of my culture and heritage until I walked about Iceland and many of my brothers and sisters there paid me the ultimate compliment of mistaking me for one of their own! This simple, seemingly insignificant, act of being mistaken for an Icelander by Icelanders, through being addressed in the beautiful Icelandic tongue so many times, has filled me with great joy.

When I heard the beautiful Icelandic language being spoken for the first time on the trip, at the airport, I cried because an empty place in my heart had been touched. Now when I hear it, I think of

Iceland, my family, and how much I love my Father.

Dad was in the habit of saying to me, "Johnny, Daddy is not going to be around forever." He said this in order to warn and prepare me for exactly what I have been going through since he died. In a sense, of course, he was right. Yet, perhaps in a more important sense, he was wrong.

Dad lives on in me, as it says in the Viking saying, as "Your work well done." For the "work" which was closest to Dad's heart was that of helping other people, especially those people who were willing to work hard and were in need of a break. He knew, along with Dickens, that "Mankind was your business." Now I hope that I might honor him by knowing, and living, the same.

Icelandic *Kaffi* with the family.

The family back home.

Cousin Stani and I with our row boat.

ABOUT THE AUTHOR

John C. Wilhelmsson is a successful businessman, author, and professor of philosophy at San Jose State University. Born and raised in San Jose he continues to reside in what he still likes to think of as "The Valley of the Heart's Delight" — Santa Clara Valley.

LOST IN THE FJORD

Nonni and his younger brother Manni are Icelandic boys who live in the charming town of Akureyri which sits by the Eyjafjörður Fjord in northern Iceland. Nonni is curious about many things yet forgetful of his parents' warnings, while Manni is quite innocent and pure of heart and loyal toward Nonni. Thinking he can lure the fish out of the sea with his magic flute playing Nonni, with trusting Manni at his side, sets out upon the Eyjafjörður Fjord in a small row boat in order to try. Great adventures follow in this classic and true story of virtue and vocation. Written by Iceland's first Jesuit priest this book features an extensive "About the Author" section. Pacific Book Review's "Best Children's Book" of 2014! (Fully illustrated and in large print).

C2OP.COM

A JOURNEY ACROSS ICELAND

Jon Sveinsson (or "Nonni") is the only Jesuit priest ever born in Iceland. He left his homeland as a boy, with his beloved brother Armann (or "Manni"), to follow their mutual call to become Jesuit missionaries. Although Manni has since passed on during his studies, Nonni is now the Reverend Jon Sveinsson S. J. The boys had wished to become Jesuit missionaries, like St. Francis Xavier, yet Jon Sveinsson has spent most of his time in the order so far as either a student, and now an instructor, in academia. Still longing to fulfill his dream of becoming a missionary he has volunteered to travel to Iceland to care for the souls of his fellow countrymen. Such is the premise of this classic Icelandic travelogue written by the man who later became one of the most beloved children's authors of all time.

C2OP.COM

www.ingramcontent.com/pod-product-compliance
Lightning Source LLC
Chambersburg PA
CBHW071125090426
42736CB00012B/2012